Excel 365 Charts

EASY EXCEL 365 ESSENTIALS - BOOK 3

M.L. HUMPHREY

CONTENTS

Introduction

This book is part of the *Easy Excel 365 Essentials* series of titles. These are targeted titles that are excerpted from the main *Excel 365 Essentials* series and are focused on one specific topic.

If you want a more general introduction to Excel, then you should check out the *Excel 365 Essentials* titles instead. In this case, *Intermediate Excel 365* which covers charts as well as a number of other topics, such as pivot tables and conditional formatting.

But if all you want is a book that covers this specific topic, then let's continue with a discussion of how to create charts in Microsoft Excel.

Charts – Basics and Types

Charts are a great way to visualize data. Sometimes numbers can be overwhelming, but a quick picture based on those numbers makes trends and patterns very clear.

Data Format

First things first, you need to format your data so that Excel can use it to create a chart.

(We'll talk about pivot tables and pivot charts later. If you work with those the pivot table basically already does this for you and then Excel knows how to build charts off of it, but I wanted to cover charts first before we have that conversation.)

For most chart types you want data labels across the top and data labels down the side, but no grand totals or sub-totals or sub-headers. Like this:

	January-2020	February-2020	April-2020	May-2020	June-2020	July-2020	August-2020	Total
Author A	$23.60	$74.26	$262.40	$296.36	$266.15	$250.00	$322.00	**$1,494.77**
Author B	$17.13	$6.88	$95.68	$3.44	$6.88	$5.59	$121.00	**$256.60**
Author C	$8.44	$6.01	$61.76	$8.98	$5.34	$1.47	$681.81	**$773.80**
Author D	$8.63	$0.52	$13.86	$22.08	$50.85	$128.46	$61.22	**$285.62**
Author E	$3.38	$0.07	$2.74	$3.47	$16.05	$11.24	$42.12	**$79.07**
Author F	$1.69	$0.06	$1.29	$1.33	$3.78	$7.14	$40.84	**$56.12**

(I usually do not include any sort of label in that top left corner, but just now when I left one there it still worked. Note this is randomly-generated data not real sales data.)

Which data label goes across the top versus down the side will impact the default chart that Excel tries to build when you choose your chart type, but there's an option to flip those if it's not how you want it in the chart, so don't worry too much about that.

If you do happen to have grand totals or labels like I do here with the Total Column, that's okay, but you'll want to select only the cells with the data and labels you want to include in your chart.

It is important that you format the data in the table you're going to use before you create your chart. I will often create charts that include a data table below the chart and when I do that the formatting of those values is directly sourced from the original data table.

So, for example, when I'm going to include a data table below my chart, I format my currency values to not have any decimal places, because it takes up too much space and that level of detail is not necessary.

Create a Chart

To create a chart, select the data you want to use for the chart and then go to the Charts section of the Insert tab and click on the dropdown for the chart type you want.

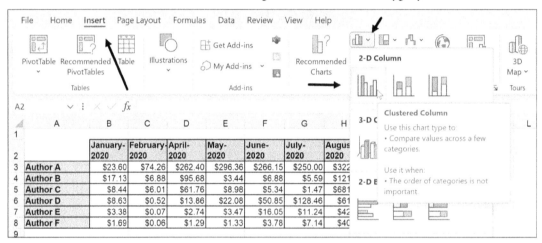

From there you'll see a list of available choices. If you hold your mouse over each one, Excel will tell you more about that specific type of chart (as you can see above for Clustered Column).

It will also create and show you the chart, but not actually insert it. If you move your mouse, the chart will disappear.

When you find the chart option you want, simply click on it and that chart will then be officially inserted into your worksheet and remain there after you move your mouse away. Charts work like equations and illustrations so are inserted on top of your worksheet, not as part of a cell. Like this:

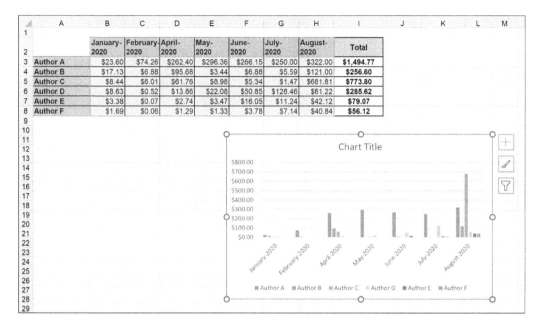

The chart is going to stay in that worksheet unless you deliberately move it, but it's on top of the cells, not embedded in them, so you can left-click and drag to move it around in the workspace without the cells being impacted.

Another option for inserting a chart is to select your data, go to the Insert tab, and then click on Recommended Charts instead. This will open the Insert Chart dialogue box and will show some recommended charts based on your data.

You can also click over to All Charts and click through there to see how your data will look with each chart type like I've done here:

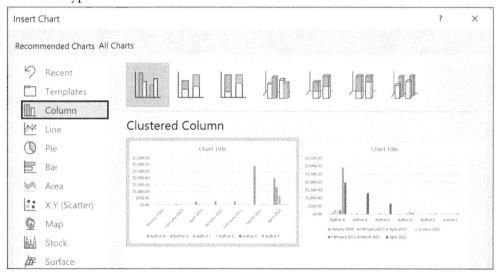

Once you find a chart you like, click on it and then click OK and it will insert.

Another option for inserting a chart is to use the Quick Analysis option. Select your data and then click on the quick analysis icon in the bottom right corner and go to Charts and you'll see some basic options there:

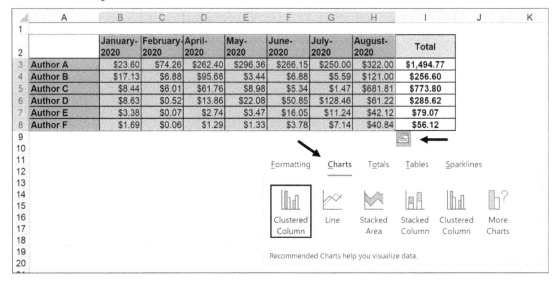

Click on any of those chart options and a chart of that type will immediately be inserted into your worksheet. Clicking on More Charts opens the Insert Chart dialogue box.

* * *

It is possible to create a chart using data that is not touching.

For example, I will sometimes have a chart like the one above that also has a totals column at the end, and want to create a chart using just that totals column. But I also need the first column to know what the values represent.

In that case, use Ctrl to select your two cell ranges, like I have here with Column A and Column I:

Just make sure that your selected ranges are the same size. I've selected Cell A2 here even though it has no data in it because I have that Total label in Cell I2 that I want to include. After that it's the same process of going to the Insert tab and making a choice. (I couldn't see the Quick Analysis option when the data I selected was not contiguous, but maybe that will change in the future.)

Which Chart

That was how to insert charts, but a big part of working with charts is figuring out which one to use. There are a few things to consider when looking at your data and making this choice. We'll walk through the type of questions you can ask yourself first and then we'll dig in and look at examples of each of the chart types mentioned.

So ask yourself…

Is there a time component to the data? For example, are you looking at sales across the months of a year?

I will, for example, use charts to look at sales for 13 months for each author name, series name, and title I publish to see if those sales are steady, increasing, or decreasing and to also compare to the same time period one year before.

For that sort of scenario, something like a bar or column chart or even a line chart is a good option. Each of those lets you visually see the changes across time periods.

Bar and column charts are better for when you have multiple variables you want to chart, like my analysis of the performance of multiple titles over the course of a year. Line charts work better with a single variable. (Although, there is a type of chart related to line charts, the area chart, that you can use for multiple variables, but at that point you're not working with a straight line, you're working with a shaded area. We'll get back to this.)

Are you instead looking to see what share of the whole each component represents? For example, at year-end I want to see what percentage of my total sales each series represented for that year. It's a snapshot of that year, I'm not looking at trends over time.

In that case something like a pie chart or doughnut chart is a good choice.

Are you trying to find a relationship between different variables? For example, how does the value of X impact the value of Y?

A scatter plot is a good choice for that one. (Excel calls them scatter charts.) You can also use a bubble chart.

Are you trying to see the distribution of a series of results. So, what's the average outcome given the data you have? In that case, a histogram can be a good choice.

There are a number of other chart types that Excel offers, but those are the ones I'm going to cover in this book. If you're curious or you need a different chart type, you can see all of them in the All Charts tab of the Insert Chart dialogue box:

Click through to see how each one will look with your data. Some of the options require a third data component or a specific format. When that's the case they won't show a preview but will instead tell you what kind of data they need. (See Stock as a good example of this.)

If you use one of those other chart types, this is a good place to open Excel's Help related to that chart and read it so you know any quirks the chart type might have. Hopefully when we're done with this discussion you'll have a solid foundation for how to insert and format any chart, but the key issue for each chart type is generally going to be making sure that you've formatted your data properly.

Okay, then. Let's now discuss our chosen chart types in more detail.

Column and Bar Charts

Column and bar charts are basically the same thing. The main difference is whether the bars are vertical (columns) or horizontal (bars.)

In the Insert Chart dialogue box they are currently listed separately, but in the Charts section of the Insert tab they are currently combined under the top leftmost choice. Here are your options:

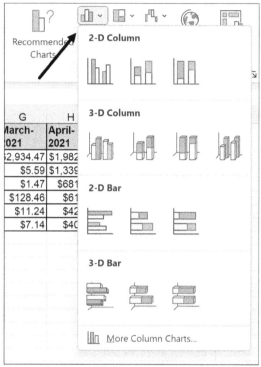

That More Column Charts choice does not in fact give you more choices, it just takes you to the Insert Chart dialogue box and gives you the same options you can see here.

The 3D options work the same as the 2D options, it's just a matter of whether you want three dimensionality or not. Since they're basically the same, I'm just going to cover your 2D choices in that first and third row.

Hold your mouse over the top of each of the three 2D choices for column or bar charts in that dropdown and you'll see that they are named clustered, stacked, and 100% stacked, respectively.

The icons for each one try to give a feel for what they look like, but we'll look at actual examples below.

Clustered column or bar charts take the results for each variable and place them side-by-side for each time period or category. For example, in the charts below we have author income for each month for six authors with a column or bar for each author for each time period, where the size of the column or bar is based on the dollar-value of the sales for that author for that time period relative to all dollar values in the data set.

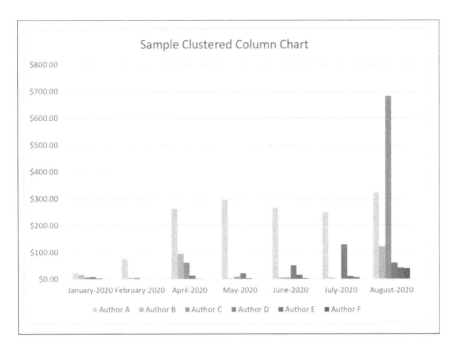

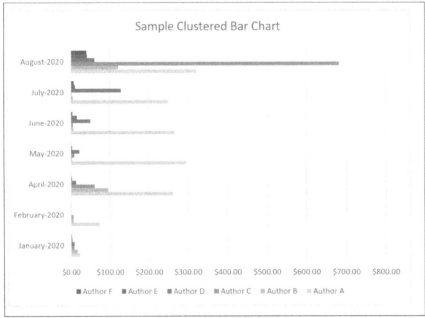

Clustered column charts can get very busy very fast so they're not the best choice when you have a large number of variables if you're also looking at a large number of time periods or categories.

Stacked column or bar charts have one column or bar per time period or category. The overall size of the column or bar for each period or category is based on the total for all variables for the period and relative to the totals for the other periods or categories. There are separate colored or shaded sections of each column or bar for each variable to show the share of the total for that variable.

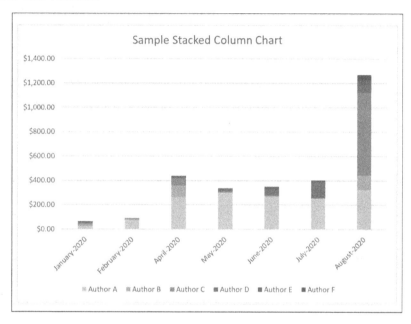

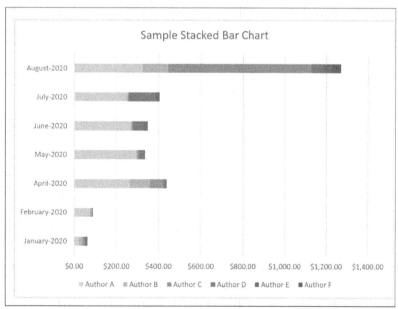

It's basically taking the individual columns or bars from a clustered chart and stacking them on top of each other.

Stacked charts are good for seeing trends over time for total performance. We can see here, for example, that August 2020 was much better than the prior months. And that January/February 2020 were much lower than the other months.

But stacked charts make it harder to see trends for the individual components that make up that whole. I can still see how Author A was dominant in most months and how Author C did really well in August 2020, but the clustered chart is better for seeing those individual-level trends.

The last bar or column chart type is the 100% stacked chart. The size of the column or bar for each time period or category is always the same, because it's always 100% of the total for that period or category.

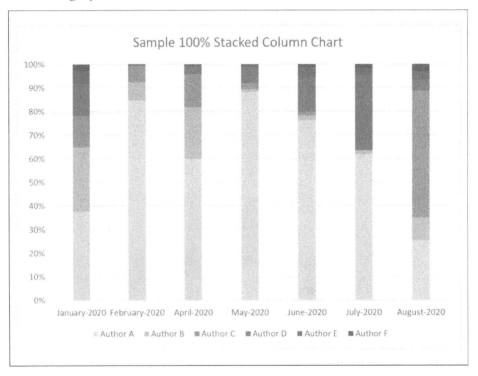

Each bar or column will be colored or shaded in sections to show the percent of the whole for each variable.

With a 100% stacked chart you lose the relative difference in actual results between time periods. Above you can see change in percentage of the whole better—we can really see that Author A dominated in all time periods—but you can't see that the first time period only had sales of $63 and the last time period had sales of $1269.

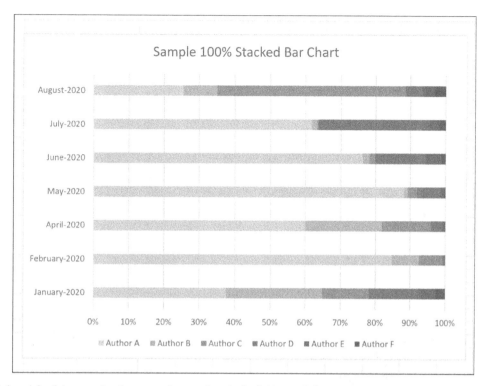

The risk with this one is that a column for $10, $40, and $50 will look the same as a column for $10,000, $40,000, and $50,000. So, if the actual amount earned in a period matters, don't rely on the 100% stacked chart for your analysis.

(One final note here, if there is a component that's a significant outlier, it can sometimes help to remove that component from the analysis so that you can better see the detail for the others. I will often drop my top-selling author or series name from my analysis to better see the results for my other authors and series.)

Pie or Doughnut Chart

As mentioned above, a pie or doughnut chart is good for a snapshot analysis where you want to see how much each variable represents of the whole. These choices are available on the left-hand side, bottom row in the Charts section of the Insert tab. Here are your choices:

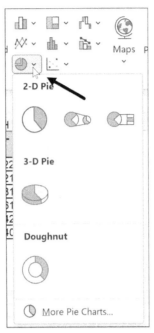

Once again, the More Pie Charts option does not actually give you more choices and I'm skipping the 3D option which has a 2D counterpart.

The data for a pie or doughnut chart is a set of labels and then a set of values, so just two columns.

Here's a basic pie chart and doughnut chart of the same data:

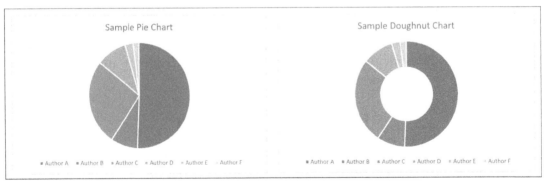

As you can see, the doughnut chart is just a hollowed-out version of the pie chart.

Both clearly show that for this data Authors A and C dominated the total share with Author A representing about half of all sales.

Those are the two main options and the ones I recommend using, but pie charts has two more options available, pie of pie and bar of pie.

These can be used to call out smaller values so that they're better visualized. BUT, if a reader is not used to seeing a chart like that, it can lead to some real confusion, in my opinion.

Let's look at the pie of pie chart for this same data to see what I'm talking about:

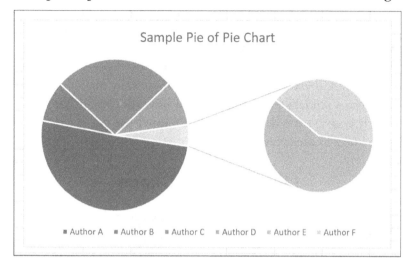

If I look at this chart without knowing how it works, I think that Author A is a big chunk of things, but then I turn to Author E in the other pie chart.

And what this is really doing is saying, "See that light blue slice of the left-hand pie? The *smallest* slice? Well that's actually two authors combined. And if we look at just those two authors in a separate pie chart, Author E has a bigger share of that small blue slice than Author F."

That right-hand pie chart that is so visible only represents 5% of the total sales. But because it gets called out this way it feels instinctively like it's a bigger share of things.

That's why if I am ever going to use one of these, I prefer the bar of pie chart, which looks like this:

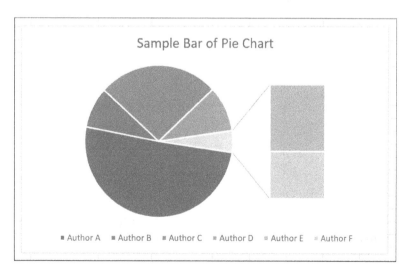

At least using a bar chart for the second chart makes it clear these are not apples to apples.

It still for me calls too much attention to those smallest values. If that slice were thirty different variables so that none of them dominated the bar chart on the right-hand side (and it's really a column, isn't it?) that might work.

But as is, with this data, I'm not a fan of using either of those charts to present this data. I'm sure they exist because there are circumstances where they make sense to use, but just be careful. Evaluate where a reader's eye might go and how they might interpret the image and whether that properly conveys the data. If it doesn't, don't use it.

Okay, now on to line and area charts.

Line and Area Charts

Line and area charts are the first chart type shown in the second row of choices in the Charts section of the Insert tab.

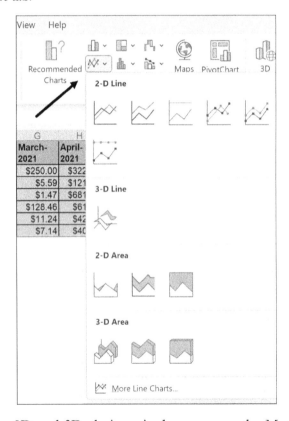

Once more we have 2D and 3D choices. And once more the More Choices option doesn't really give you more choices. The Insert Charts dialogue box has the choices you see here split between Line and Area charts.

Be sure here, and really with any data that has a time component to it, that your data is sorted in order. It can't be randomly listed in your data table.

I want to start by looking at the first option there which is the basic Line chart:

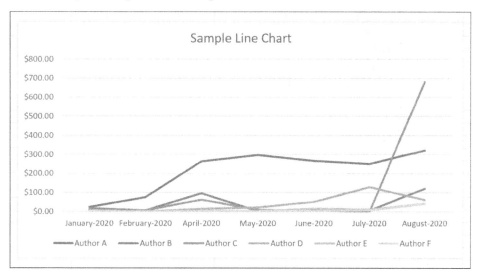

You can see here that very clear spike from Author C in August 2020. And you can see how Author A went up at the start and then plateaued at a level above the rest for most of the period.

Line charts are good for seeing a linear trend across time periods or categories. But they are not good for situations where you only have one or two data points. If I had a new author start selling in August 2020 there'd be no line to draw.

Here I've dropped Author C to better see the trend for the other authors and also changed the chart type to Line With Markers:

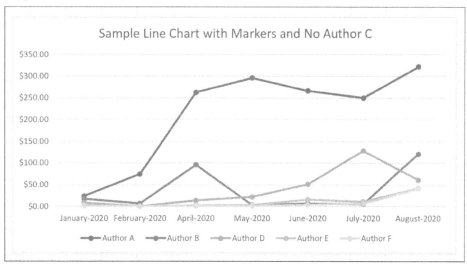

The line chart with markers option is the fourth listed choice. (It used to be that in older versions of Excel this lined up nicely so it was the first option on the second row, but that's no longer the case. Just think of it as the first of the options that shows markers, those dots on the line that represent specific data points.)

Using a line chart that includes markers for each data point can sometimes be helpful because it better shows where there's an actual data point versus where it's just a line connecting two points. The more markers between two points, the more faith you can have that the data actually followed that path.

Here, for example, is the data we've seen already for Authors A, B, and C for each month from January to August 2020 in the left-hand chart. In the right-hand chart we just have the data for January and for August.

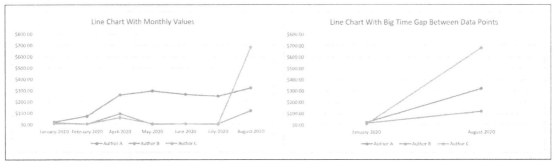

For Author A, I have more faith that the change in earnings from January to August followed a steady pattern given the number of results in the first chart because there are six data points charting that rise versus just one in the second chart.

We can also see here how the second chart with just a beginning and an ending observation hides how Author C basically didn't perform at all until the final time period.

Basically, the more data, the better, and markers can be an indicator of how much data there was.

Those are the two line charts I recommend because they are what people traditionally expect of line charts. Each line is showing the values for that line and is separate from the other lines.

The other line chart options shown there are stacked and 100% stacked line charts. They act like the stacked and 100% stacked bar and column charts, meaning the lines are building upon one another to reach a total value for the period or to reach 100% for each period. But it's just not intuitive to most users that that's what they're seeing, so I don't recommend using them.

Here's the stacked line chart for this data, for example:

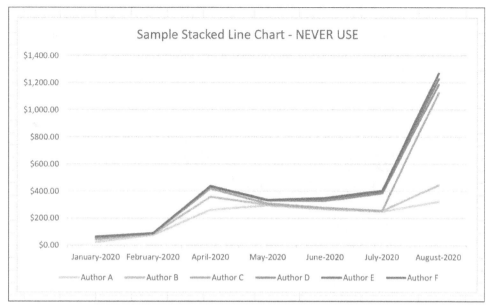

See what I mean? You just automatically assume that those lines are the results for each Author because that's how we're used to interpreting lines on charts. Or at least *I* do.

Area charts fix this issue. You've probably seen one or two over the last couple years, because they're used often with epidemiological data.

Here are the two area charts I recommend using applied to this data:. The first is the Stacked Area chart:

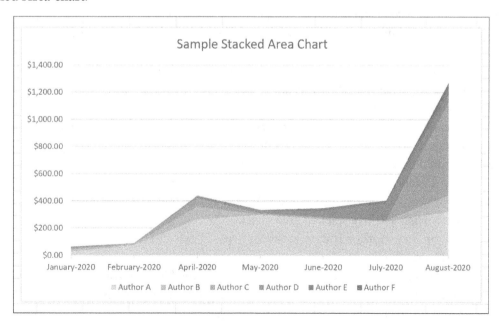

See how filling in the space between the lines gives the overall image cohesion? You can more readily understand that the various filled-in areas are adding up to something instead of representing separate results when the spaces between the lines are filled in.

The second is the 100% stacked area chart:

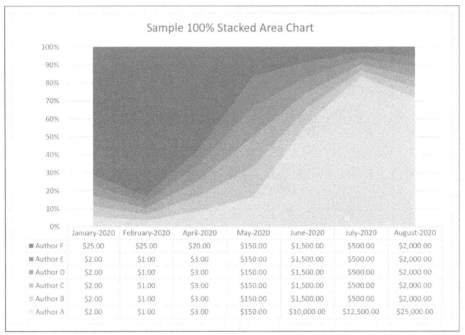

	January-2020	February-2020	April-2020	May-2020	June-2020	July-2020	August-2020
■ Author F	$25.00	$25.00	$20.00	$150.00	$1,500.00	$500.00	$2,000.00
■ Author E	$2.00	$1.00	$3.00	$150.00	$1,500.00	$500.00	$2,000.00
■ Author D	$2.00	$1.00	$3.00	$150.00	$1,500.00	$500.00	$2,000.00
■ Author C	$2.00	$1.00	$3.00	$150.00	$1,500.00	$500.00	$2,000.00
■ Author B	$2.00	$1.00	$3.00	$150.00	$1,500.00	$500.00	$2,000.00
■ Author A	$2.00	$1.00	$3.00	$150.00	$10,000.00	$12,500.00	$25,000.00

Be careful with the 100% stacked option, because it can give a misleading impression of the overall share of the results across time as you can see with the data I created for use in this one.

If you just look at the chart without the data, you would think that Author F and Author A just switched places. One was dominant early and then the other took over, but they basically had equal shares overall.

Which is true percentage-wise. Early on Author F was doing 2.5 times what all the other authors were doing combined. And at the end Author A was doing the same.

But what you'd completely miss from this chart (without the data table included) is that Author F made a grand total of $4,220 for the period covered by the chart and Author A made $47,656. Author A made *ten times* more than Author F, but that's completely hidden when you present the data using a 100% stacked area chart.

As a matter of fact, Author F who looks so great in this chart only earned $64 more than Authors B, C, D, and E.

Not obvious from what we see here because it's showing % share for each time period. The problem is that the use of a shaded area that crosses time periods makes the data feel connected when it's really not. At least not in that way.

The 100% stacked bar and column charts don't have this issue because each column or bar is discrete so they do a better job of reminding a viewer that the percentages are for that time period or category only.

Hope that makes sense. Basically, if you have wide swings in your actual results between time periods, do not use the 100% Stacked Area chart. It's misleading.

Okay, then. On to scatter plots.

Scatter and Bubble Plots

Scatter plots take two inputs and plot them on a grid to make a data point. A scatter plot can connect those data points to see if there's some sort of relationship between the two inputs, but it doesn't have to.

The scatter plot dropdown is the last one, on the bottom row, next to pie charts.

There are five options:

The first one just plots the points. The other options allow you to add either a smoothed line or a straight line that connects the points. The line can either show markers for the data points or not.

Here is a small data table with the data points plotted but not connected.

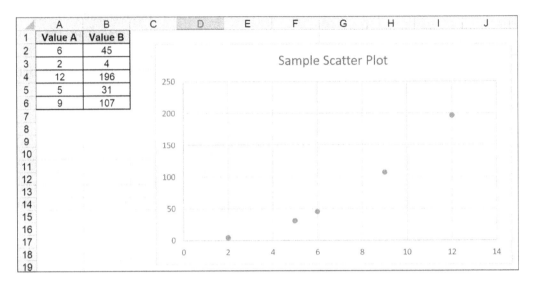

You can see that there's probably a relationship there, right? When one value goes up, so does the other. It's not perfectly linear, but it's there. (I created it so I know it's there.)

Now, here's the tricky thing with scatter plots. If I add a line connecting my data points Excel will draw that line by connecting the first point to the second point to the third point and on and on.

Here I used the smooth line option with markers:

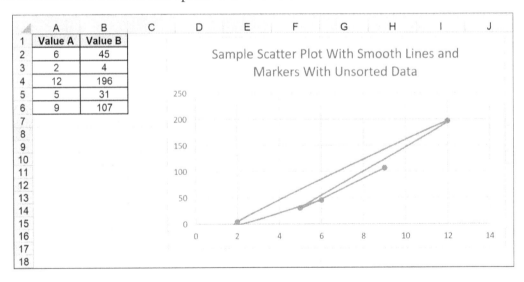

That's a hot mess, isn't it? Why?

Because while there is a relationship between Value A and Value B, it's one that's independent of the order in which the observations were made.

If I sort my data by value, now we see it:

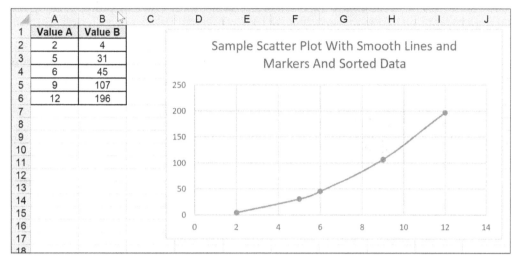

The data points didn't change. It's just the order in which they were connected that changed.

Whether you should sort the data in your plot like I just did or not is going to depend on what the data is and why it was in that order.

You can also plot multiple sets of data in the same scatter plot. The first column of data will drive the values on the x axis (the bottom) and then any other columns of data will be plotted against the y axis (the side).

Here, for example, I have three columns of data (Columns B, C, and D) plotted against the values in Column A.

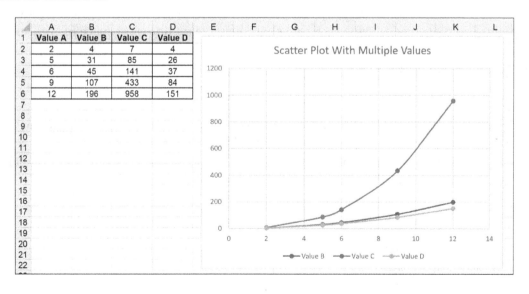

You don't have to use lines when you do this, the data points for each column will have their own color, but I recommend it. It makes it easier to see which points belong to each column.

Above you can see that there is a relationship between the values in Column A and the values in Columns B, C, and D, but that that relationship is not the same. Here I've edited the values for Column C so there is no clear linear, quadratic, or binomial relationship:

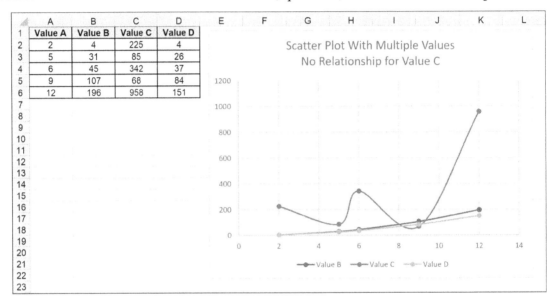

The line goes up and down and not in any apparent pattern.

In the same dropdown as scatter plots, you can also see bubble plots. A bubble plot takes two points and plots them against each other and then it takes one more piece of information and uses that to determine the size of the data point so you end up with three pieces of information shown for each data point.

Often you'll see this with country GDP, for example. So the original plot is spending versus population but then the size of the bubble is the overall "wealth" of the country. Or percent of population that adopted some health measure versus an outcome for that measure with the size of each data point showing per capita income. That sort of thing.

Here is a basic example, using the same data as our original scatter plot, but now with a number of observations column added to dictate the bubble size.

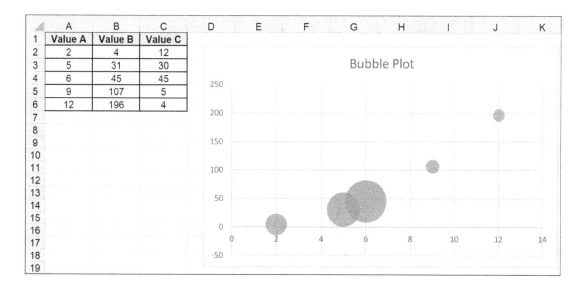

▲	A	B	C	D	E	F	G	H	I	J	K
1	**Value A**	**Value B**	**Value C**								
2	2	4	12								
3	5	31	30								
4	6	45	45								
5	9	107	5								
6	12	196	4								

This lets us see that the majority of the data is centered around two values for A, 5 and 6, which makes me less confident that the apparent pattern in this data exists since the data that is on the far left and on the far right is much less robust. (One outlier data point can sometimes skew your data in weird ways.) But there's still a handful of observations for each data point so it probably does exist. The bubble chart just lets me know to be more cautious with values for A that are further away from 5 or 6.

Okay. That was scatter and bubble plots. I used to use them a lot in physics class and economics, but one I actually use for my writing is the histogram. So let's talk about that one next.

Histogram

The histogram chart was a recent addition to Excel. It lets you take your data and create buckets of observations that are close in value and then plots a count of how many observations are in each bucket.

So instead of treating 31, 32, 33, and 34 as separate values, it might group those all into a 30 to 40 bucket. This can be nice because it removes the noise in your data and lets you better see any patterns.

The histogram option is in the middle of the chart choices and requires one column of values. Here I've created a histogram from randomly generated values between 0 and 100.

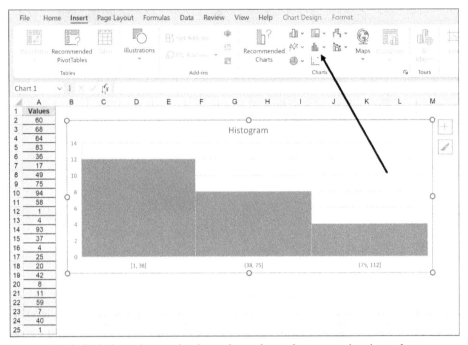

The histogram by default is going to look at the values that you give it and come up with the buckets it places those values into. In this case it used three buckets, 1 to 38, 38 to 75, and 75 to 112.

The height of each bar is based on the number of values that fall into that bucket. You can see that right now the 1 to 38 bucket contains the most values with 12 observations.

You can manually choose how many buckets to use and how wide they are in the formatting task pane (which we'll discuss in detail shortly.) For a histogram this is under Horizontal Axis, Axis Options, and then the Axis Options section. Here I've changed the number of bins (buckets) to ten and capped the histogram between 0 and 100.

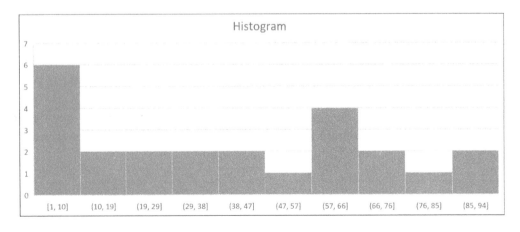

As you can see it definitely impacts where we think most results will fall. Also, interestingly enough because I know how this data was created, we clearly don't have enough data points yet to see the true pattern in this data.

I added more observations and plotted again:

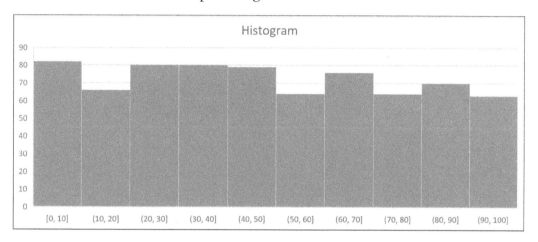

This is far closer to the true data pattern behind these values but still not quite there. Which is a reminder to always exercise caution in interpreting data when there aren't enough observations yet.

Okay, that was the last of the chart types I wanted to cover in more detail. We'll cover pivot charts when we cover pivot tables. They'll use these same chart types, the main difference is basically where the data is coming from.

For now, though, let's talk about all the bells and whistles you can add to a chart and how to edit charts to make them look exactly how you want. (Some of which I've been doing behind the scenes already.)

Charts – Editing and Formatting

If you look back at the screenshots I showed you in the last section you will notice that the charts have descriptive titles that tell you what type of chart it is. And that some of the charts are different sizes or shapes and that they don't use the default color palette.

That's because I edited them. There are a large number of edits you can make to charts.

Let me start with those basic things I did in the last section and then we'll go through more systematically.

Resize a Chart

To resize a chart, click on the chart. You will then see big circles appear at each corner and in the middle of each side of the chart. Like this:

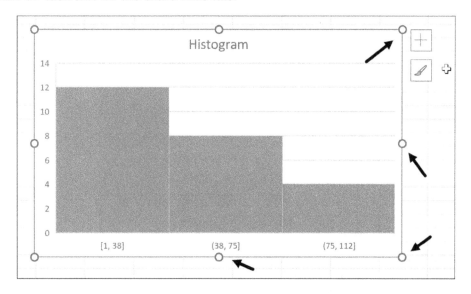

Left-click on one of those circles and drag to change the size of your chart.

To resize both the top and side at once, click and drag from one of the corners. If you do so at an angle, the chart should resize proportionately. All of the elements within the chart space should also resize to fit the new dimensions.

I find resizing charts essential when I include data tables with my charts like I did in one of the examples above. And I usually use this click and drag method because I'm a visual person so I want to resize to what "looks right".

But you can also go to the Format tab that appears for your chart when you click on it and on the far right-hand side you'll see a Size section where you can type in a new value for height, width, or both. Just click into each box and type your new value.

That expansion arrow in the corner of the Size section will open the task pane for Format Chart Area where you can also enter specific values. Clicking on Lock Aspect Ratio will make sure that any change you make to one value (height or width) will also be reflected in the other value (width or height) so that the proportion of width to height remains the same.

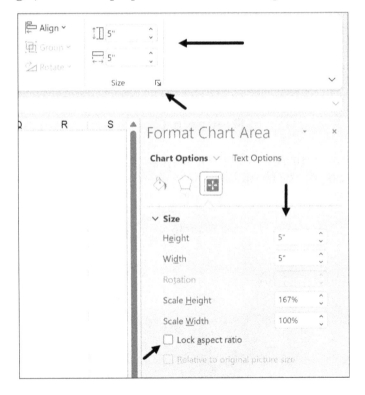

Move a Chart

You can also move a chart from where Excel places it. Left-click on the chart and drag to move it to a new location in your workspace. Be careful when you click on the chart that you click somewhere on the chart that doesn't have a chart element, like the title. Because if you click on a chart element you may end up moving the element around instead of the chart.

Charts can also be copied or cut and pasted using the Ctrl shortcuts (Ctrl + C, Ctrl + X, Ctrl + V) or the menu options. This is how I normally move them.

If you right-click and choose Move Chart from the dropdown menu it will show you a dialogue box that will let you move the chart to a different worksheet or a new worksheet. If you choose to move to a new worksheet it will be one that has no cells in it. And you can't undo that move or cut the chart from that worksheet, so the only way to put the chart back in its original location is to right-click and choose to move it again and then select the original worksheet as the location.

The Move Chart option can also be found in the Location section of the Chart Design tab.

When you move a chart to a new worksheet, workbook, or other Office document, your data does not move, only the chart does. (Which is usually what you want, but something to be aware of regardless.) Depending on how you pasted the chart it may still be impacted by any changes to that source data.

Change the Chart Title

To change the title of your chart, click on the name of the chart. Click again on the name to see your cursor blinking amidst the text. Select the text for the current name and then type in what you want to use. (If you want to replace the entire title, Ctrl + A will highlight the current title which will be replaced when you start typing.)

Move Elements Within a Chart

You can move the elements in a chart by clicking on them and then left-clicking and dragging or clicking on a circle in one of the corners to change the shape or size. If an element in a chart can be moved or have its size/shape changed, it will show that frame with circles.

Change A Field Name Used in the Legend

The best bet is to do this in the actual data table that is the source of the data used in the chart. But if that's not possible, use the Select Data option in the Chart Design tab. In the Select Data Source dialogue box, click on the field name, then click on Edit. In the Edit Series or Axis Labels dialogue box that appears, type in the new name in the Series Name or Axis Label Range field.

* * *

Chart Design Tab Options

Okay. Those were the quick basics that I almost always need. Now let's be more systematic about this and walk through the editing options in the Chart Design tab (which can be found to the right of the Help tab when you click on a chart).

Let's start with those options there on the right-hand side, Switch Row/Column, Select Data, and Change Chart Type.

Switch Row/Column

This is the one that makes it irrelevant which data you put across the top or down the side in your data table for a standard bar/column chart or line graph. Because if you find when you create your chart that the wrong variable is along the bottom or the wrong variable is shown in the main chart space, you can flip them using this.

If you use the Insert Chart dialogue box to insert your charts you probably will never even need to do this, because that way of inserting charts shows you both choices:

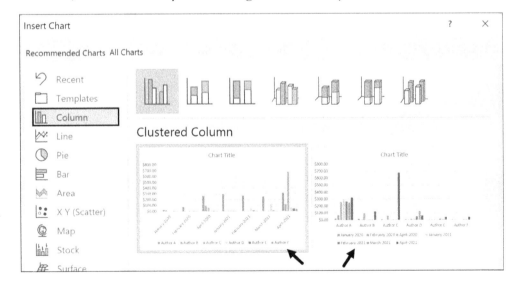

It may be a little hard to see, but the two clustered column choices in the screenshot above have different X axis values. One is showing months on the X axis and then plotting the data by author name for each of those months. The other is showing author names on the X axis and then plotting the data by month for each author name.

Clicking that Switch Row/Column button basically moves you between those two choices.

It's only available when there is data to switch (all of the chart types we discussed except for histograms have it available) and it sometimes won't make any sense to use it (for pie and doughnut charts for example).

Select Data

The Select Data option opens the Select Data Source dialogue box.

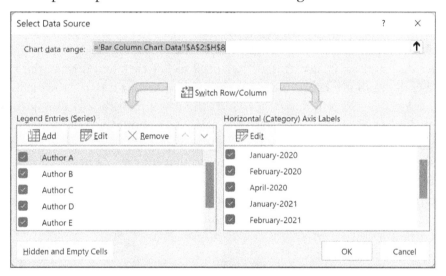

You can do a number of things here.

First, you can switch row/column by clicking on that option in the center of the dialogue box.

Second, you can uncheck the boxes for any of the inputs to the x- or y-axis to exclude them from the chart. This is where I would go to drop Author A, for example, if Author A's data was dominating a chart and I couldn't adequately see the other results.

Third, as mentioned above, you can click on Edit and edit the name for each series of data if you can't edit that name in the data table that's the source for the chart.

And, fourth, you can change the range of the data that's being used by clicking into the Chart Data Range field and changing the cell notation to your new data range.

I prefer to change my data range in the data table itself, however, so let me walk you through how to do that real quick.

First step is to click onto the chart that's using that data table. That will highlight the cells in your data table that are being used by that chart.

Here I have a data table that shows sales for Authors A through F, but if you look at the data table only the data for Authors A through E is highlighted.

	A	B	C	D	E	F	G	H	I
1									
2		January-2020	February-2020	April-2020	May-2020	June-2020	July-2020	August-2020	Total
3	Author A	$23.60	$74.26	$262.40	$296.36	$266.15	$250.00	$322.00	$1,494.77
4	Author B	$17.13	$6.88	$95.68	$3.44	$6.88	$5.59	$121.00	$256.60
5	Author C	$8.44	$6.01	$61.76	$8.98	$5.34	$1.47	$681.81	$773.80
6	Author D	$8.63	$0.52	$13.86	$22.08	$50.85	$128.46	$61.22	$285.62
7	Author E	$3.38	$0.07	$2.74	$3.47	$16.05	$11.24	$42.12	$79.07
8	Author F	$1.69	$0.06	$1.29	$1.33	$3.78	$7.14	$40.8	$56.12
9									

The cells that are being used are shaded differently and there is a colored line around them indicating which part of the chart those cells populate.

To expand the chart to include Author F, I need to left-click and drag in the bottom right corner of either the Author E cell or the last sales entry for Author E (see arrows in image above).

That will bring the selection down to include the row for Author F. Doing either the cell that contains Author E or that last cell with sales data should select the entire next row, including the author name and author sales data for Author F. (If it doesn't, you'll have to do them both separately. I want to say that I have to do that for my line graph of sales, ad spend, and profit, for example.)

When your mouse is appropriately positioned, the cursor should be an angled line with arrows on each end. It's a little hard to see, but here's a screenshot of what that looks like:

	A	B	C	D	E
3	Author A	$23.60	$74.26	$262.40	$296.36
4	Author B	$17.13	$6.88	$95.68	$3.44
5	Author C	$8.44	$6.01	$61.76	$8.98
6	Author D	$8.63	$0.52	$13.86	$22.08
7	Author E	$3.38	$0.07	$2.74	$3.47
8	Author F	$1.69	$0.06	$1.29	$1.33
9					

Once your mouse looks like that, just left-click and drag to select the rest of the data you need. (Note that you can also drag upward if you want to use less data in your chart, but usually I'm adding more data using this method.)

Okay. So to recap: click on the chart, find the edge of the current data range, left-click and drag to make it include my other cells.

But, as mentioned, you can also do so by editing the text in the Select Data dialogue box.

Change Chart Type

To change the chart type for an existing chart, click on the chart, and then click on this option. It brings up the Change Chart dialogue box which is identical to the Insert Chart dialogue box. Click on the new chart type you want and then choose OK.

* * *

Okay, now let's move on to the formatting options on the left-hand side of the Chart Design tab:

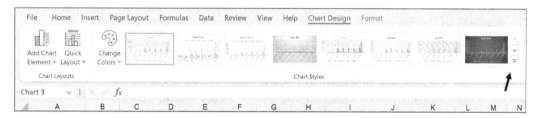

Chart Styles

I'm going to continue working right to left because that final option (Add Chart Element) is going to be a doozy.

Chart Styles are pre-formatted styles that you can apply to your chart. They will vary based upon what kind of chart you use. Click on the downpointing arrow in the bottom right corner (noted in the screenshot above) to expand the selections list and see all available options at once, like here where there are fourteen possible column chart styles available:

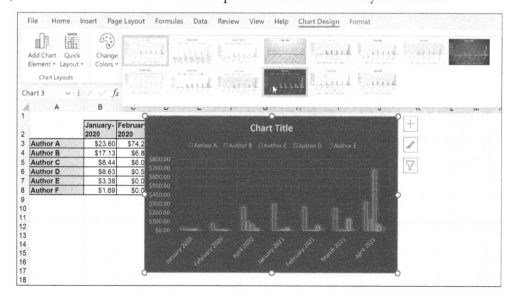

You can also just use the up and down arrows on the right-hand side to see more options (if there are any).

Hold your mouse over each option to see it applied to your chart.

Above I'm looking at one with a black background and different outline and fill color used for each column.

For me personally these styles never are what I want. But they can be a good way to get close to what you want and then tweak from there.

Change Colors

The change colors dropdown allows you to change from Excel's default color scheme, which for me has blue, orange, gray, and yellow for the first four choices, to one of the color schemes shown in the dropdown.

I actually did this for the charts in the last section because I wanted to make sure that a black and white image of that chart in the print books would still have clear differences between the different variables in each chart.

The monochromatic options all work for that. I went with a blue choice so that the ebooks would still have color in them, but I could have chosen monochromatic palettes 3, 7, or 10 if I wanted to only use shades of gray and black.

As with Chart Styles, you can hold your mouse over each choice and see what it will look like before you make your selection by clicking on it.

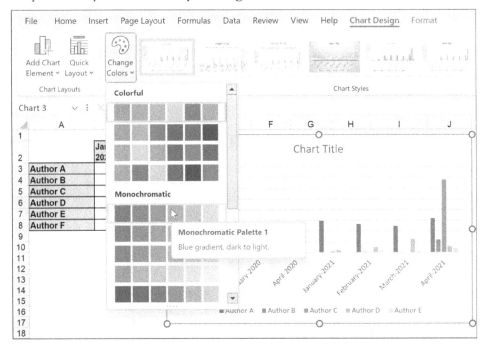

Quick Layout

The quick layout dropdown is another one that shows different potential layouts for your data and will vary based on chart type. It doesn't include different formatting like the Chart Styles do, but is more about including different chart elements.

You can hold your mouse over each one to see it applied and see what it's supposed to include:

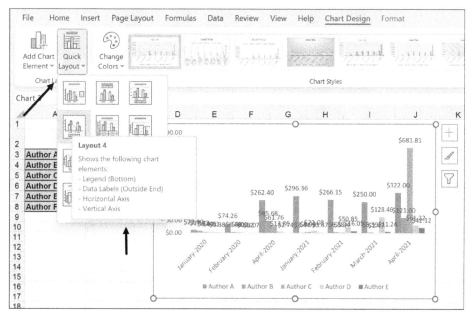

Even when the option is ugly, like this one above, it can give you an idea of which chart elements you may want in your own chart.

Click on the option if you want to keep it.

Be careful if you want to use both Quick Layout and Chart Style because they may overwrite one another. Quick Layout will keep the colors of a Chart Style but may change other elements. Chart Style can sometimes appear to completely replace a Quick Layout, but not always. So the best bet is to see where you end up at the end and use Ctrl + Z if needed to undo.

Or you can get ideas from both of them and then add your own chart elements and formatting, which we'll discuss now, starting with the chart elements.

Add Chart Element

This is where I do most of my chart editing. I almost always want a data table under the chart which means I also remove the chart legend. And I also like to use trendlines sometimes.

To see the list of available Chart Elements, click on the dropdown arrow next to Add Chart Element.

The available options vary by chart type since not all chart types can use all of the chart elements listed. Grayed-out elements are not available for that chart type, like here where Lines and Up/Down Bars are not available options.

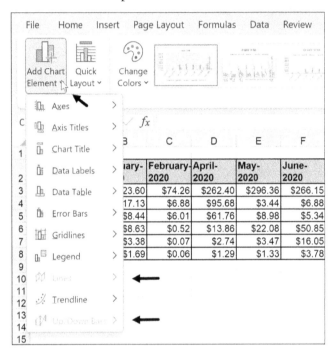

Each element will have a secondary dropdown with the choices for that element. Hold your mouse over the element name to see the available options and then hold your mouse over each choice to see it applied temporarily to your chart. Click on the choice to apply it permanently.

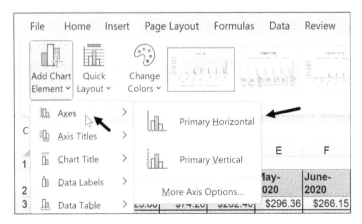

Here you can see the choices for Axes, Primary Horizontal and Primary Vertical.

Clicking on the More [X] Options choice at the bottom of the dropdown opens the task pane for formatting that element, which is where the most options are available.

Now let's walk through each option and what it does:

Axes

Axes allows you to add or remove the data point labels on each axis. For example, I sometimes will share a line chart of sales data on my blog but I don't feel the need to share the dollar values involved or sometimes even the months covered by that data, so I remove those labels from my chart.

Here I have removed the $ values from the y-axis and months from the x-axis but the overall trends across periods are still clear.

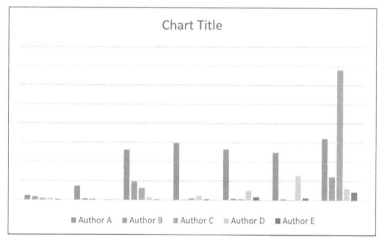

(If this were a chart I was going to share with others I'd need to change the title so others would know what is being plotted here. Something like "Author Revenues Over Time.")

Axis Titles

Axis titles are the text that tells you what each axis contains. You can add or remove them through this menu option.

By default they are not applied. Adding one creates a text box with the text "Axis Title". You then need to edit that text to whatever descriptor you want to use. See below for an example of a chart with an axis title (Months Covered).

Chart Title

The chart title option lets you add, move, or remove a chart title.

There is one present by default that is centered above the chart. You can also place the chart title in a centered overlay position where it's in the center but on the contents of the chart. Like so:

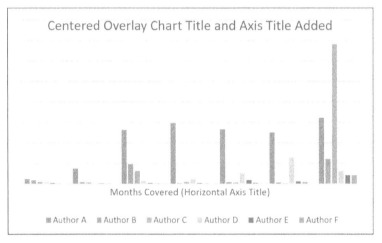

See how the horizontal gridlines run behind the text? With the Above Chart option, they'd all be below the title.

Data Labels

Data labels show the specific value for each data point. They are not present by default.

With most charts you can hold your mouse over any column, bar, data point, pie slice, etc. to see the actual specific value for that data point, even when it's not visible on the chart itself.

But sometimes you want the values showing on the chart. I find this particularly necessary with pie charts which are showing a percentage share because I also want to know the dollar value for that data point.

Here is a pie chart with data labels using the Outside End option:

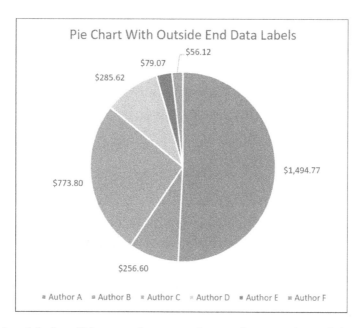

Sometimes two data labels will be too close together and you can't read them because they're on top of each other. That happened in the image above with the $79.07 and $56.12 at the top of the pie chart.

To fix that, click on the data label you want to move and then left-click and drag to move it to a better position. Excel will add a line from the data label to the element it's associated with so you can still see which label belongs to which element in the chart. (You can see that above with the $56.12.)

Data Table

This is one I use often. It places a table below the chart of all of the values that were used to create the chart. I always choose the "with legend keys" choice because that lets me get rid of the legend. If you use that option, the data table can serve both purposes.

When I add one of these, I almost always need to increase the height of the table to show all of the data. Depending on how much data you're including, the data table can at times be bigger than the chart itself.

Also, it's important when using a data table to think about the format of your data in the source data table. I often will format that data in the source table to remove the cents portion of my values so they take up less room.

Error Bars

Error bars lets you add bars to your chart that show standard error, standard deviation, or percentage error in your data. You can also customize the error bars in the task pane to show what a X% error range would be for that data point. If you're curious about how Excel calculates the values, see the Help text for error bars. This is one I recommend you only use if you know what you're doing.

Gridlines

Gridlines are those lines that run behind the chart space that let you more easily track from a data point to its value along an axis. If you want more lines than you're seeing on the chart, you can add minor lines. The default is usually major horizontal lines.

Legend

The legend is what tells you which color in the chart goes with which variable. You can add or remove a legend using this option and you can also choose whether the legend is displayed on the top, bottom, left, or right of the chart.

I definitely recommend having one if you don't have a data table with legends included and there's more than one primary variable shown in the chart. (When in doubt preview it and see if it helps.) Legends are generally included by default in chart types that need them.

Lines

The lines option allows you to add high-low lines or drop lines to a line chart. High-low lines basically connect the highest and lowest value for a time period or observation. Drop lines go from the highest value down to the axis. If you need them you probably know how to use them.

Trendline

A trendline looks at your values and estimates an overall line that shows the direction of those values. This is one I like to use often for things like profit and loss or revenue.

If you have multiple lines in a chart, you have to add one trendline per line. It will by default be a dotted line in the same color as the line it's related to.

Be careful choosing which type of trendline to add. Your choices are linear, exponential, linear forecast, and moving average.

In this chart below I have four trendlines, two each for Authors A and B.

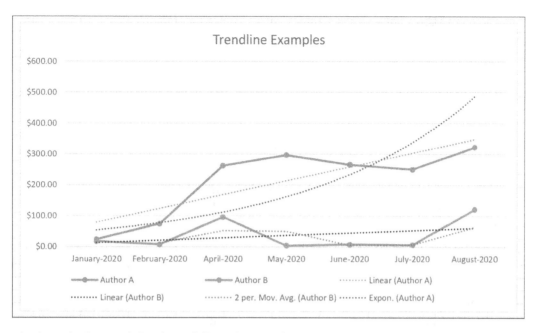

For Author A the straight dotted line that's colored blue is a linear trendline. The curved dotted line that's colored purple is an exponential line.

Of the two, the straight dotted line is the better fit, because Excel doesn't allow a logarithmic trendline choice which is what would likely best fit this data.

For Author B the dark purple dotted line is the linear trendline and the red dotted line that goes up and down is the moving average trendline.

While the linear trendline is close at the beginning and end points, it has no relationship whatsoever to the points in between. This is not linear data. The moving average line doesn't help much either. Although it does better fit the results than the linear line.

Sometimes trendlines help, sometimes they don't. You have to see your data plotted first to decide.

Up/Down Bars

Up/Down Bars connect the first data series data point to the last data series data point.

These get added by default in stock charts.

* * *

Customize Formatting

Okay. So that was a discussion of the various elements you can add or remove from a chart.

Now let's talk about how to customize your formatting. We're going to start with the Format tab that's available when you click on a chart. The formatting options are located in the middle of that Format tab:

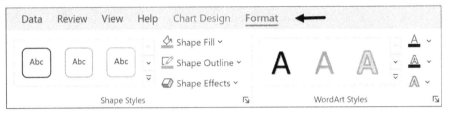

Shape Styles are preformatted styles that use different outline colors, interior colors and formats, and text colors (white or black, depending). Click on the downward pointing arrow to see all of the available styles at once. You'll mostly use these for the chart elements like columns or bars, but they can also be applied to text boxes, such as the one around a chart title.

WordArt Styles are for text and involve various text effects such as shadows, beveling, outline colors, fill colors, and patterns. (I don't recommend using them, to be honest.)

In addition, to the right side of both Shape Styles and WordArt Styles are options for fill, outline, and effects that allow you to completely customize the appearance of the shape and text elements in your chart.

To apply these formats to a chart element, you first need to select the element in the chart that you want to format.

So if I want to convert my blue column to a different color, I'd click on one example of that blue column in the chart. That should select all other instances of the blue column. They'll all be outlined and have those circles at the corners like you can see here:

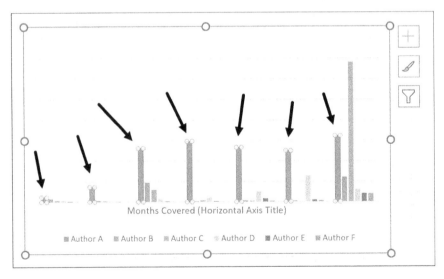

Once all instances of an element are selected, you can then click on the formatting option you want to apply. Holding your mouse over an option will temporarily apply it. Click to permanently apply it.

In this case, if I wanted to apply a different color to that column I could use the Shape Fill dropdown menu to choose a new color.

Or here, for example, I'm holding my mouse over a Shape Style that uses a white fill color with a green outline and you can see it applied to those five columns in the background.

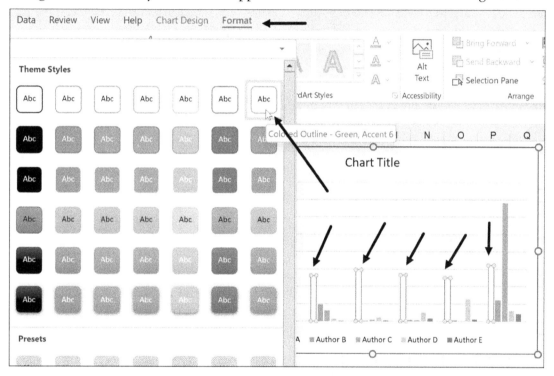

A few more tips on using these options.

With pie and doughnut charts, make sure that you only select one slice or section. It's very easy to select them all at once for some reason, so check which slices are outlined before you apply a format. Usually, I have to click on the slice or section I want to format twice to make sure it's the only one selected.

Use Shape Fill to change the color of columns, bars, pie wedges, etc. Use Shape Outline to change the color of lines.

You can use both shape fill and shape outline on columns, bars, etc. to give a border color around a shape that is different from the interior, like we saw above with the green outline and white fill.

If the fill color is not white, the border may not be obvious. You can adjust the line weight using the Weight option in the Shape Outline dropdown menu. (Unlike with borders, you don't have to adjust the weight first before applying the color. As long as the elements are still selected, you can adjust the line weight at any point in time.)

In addition to color changes and line weight, the dropdowns for fill, outline, and effects allow a number of other formatting choices like adding a gradient or texture, using a picture, adding edges and shadows, etc.

Feel free to explore them. Just be sure if you go down that path that you're not overwhelming the data in the chart with weird formatting. There can be a tendency for newer users to get so excited with all the bells and whistles that Excel offers that they lose the point of what they're doing.

A chart is meant to effectively convey information about complex data in a simple and intuitive manner. If the formatting you add to a chart is not helping do that, don't use it.

That's why I'm not going to go into more detail here on these formatting options, because you can do all sorts of things to your shapes and text in your chart, but you probably shouldn't.

* * *

Chart Task Pane

We've touched on the chart task pane with respect to charts a few times now, but I wanted to address it specifically.

The chart task pane is definitely the most thorough option for formatting a chart. And if you want to, you can start with it when you decide to format.

(I don't use it by default because I don't think it's as intuitive to use as the Format tab.)

To open the task pane, right-click on your chart and choose the Format [X] option towards the bottom of the dropdown menu.

What option is listed will vary depending on where you are on the chart when you right-click. For example, I had various choices like Format Data Series, Format Gridlines, Format Plot Area, Format Chart Area, etc.

Any of those will open the chart task pane on the right-hand side of your worksheet.

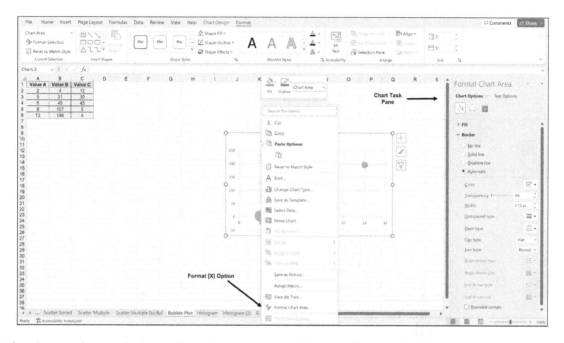

The chart task pane is dynamic so the task pane you see will depend on where you were in the chart when you opened it. You can change what you're seeing using the dropdown arrow next to that top options header, which in this case is Chart Options:

Above, for example, we have the option to change it to edit settings related to the chart area, chart title, horizontal axis, legend, plot area, etc.

Each task pane has icons at the top that you can click on to see various options. Hold your mouse over the icon to see what it covers. Here, for example, the middle icon is for effects:

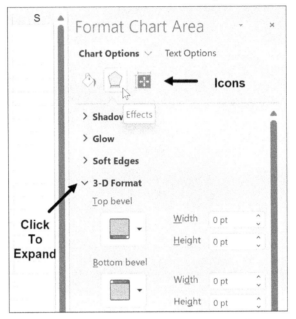

When you click on one of those icons, the pane will show various categories of settings. So above you can see Shadow, Glow, Soft Edges, and 3-D Format. Click on the arrow to the left of each category to expand it and see the settings for that category like I have above for 3-D Format.

The chart task pane is the only way I know where you can "explode" a pie chart. If you explode a pie chart you take the individual slices and move them outward from the center so that there's more space between them.

To do this, click on the pie chart portion of the pie chart and then right-click and choose Format Data Series to open the task pane. Change the task pane settings until you are in Series Options and have clicked on the third icon which is also Series Options. Pie explosion is the setting at the bottom. Use the slider or change the percentage to "explode" the pie until there's enough space between the slices for what you wanted.

This is a pie chart with a 10% explosion setting:

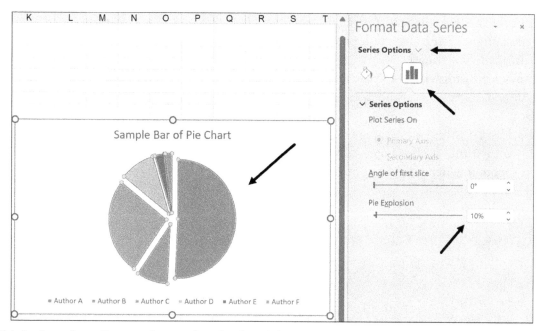

This is also where I go to change the pie chart labels to % values. This can be done in the Label Options section. (Label Options, Label Options, uncheck the box for Value and check the box for Percentage.)

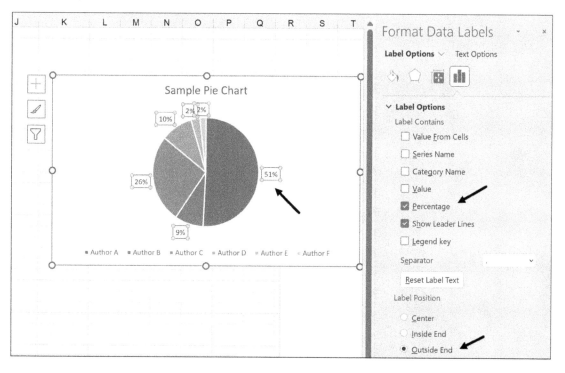

In this case, I did have to add labels using the Chart Design tab first. That could just be my unfamiliarity with the chart task pane, but it seems to only provide options for elements that are already in your chart.

Also, for histograms the chart task pane is the only way I know to customize the bins. As mentioned above, that's under Horizontal Axis, Axis Options, and then the Axis Options section.

Basically, if there's something you want to do with a chart that you think should be possible and you can't find it elsewhere, it's probably somewhere in the chart task pane. (Also, try the Help function which is pretty robust for charts.)

Appendix A: Basic Terminology

These terms are defined in detail in *Excel 365 for Beginners*. This is just a quick overview in case it's needed.

Workbook

A workbook is what Excel likes to call an Excel file.

Worksheet

Excel defines a worksheet as the primary document you use in Excel to store and work with your data. A worksheet is organized into Columns and Rows that form Cells. A workbook can contain multiple worksheets.

Columns

Excel uses columns and rows to display information. Columns run across the top of the worksheet and, unless you've done something funky with your settings, are identified using letters of the alphabet.

The first column in a worksheet will always be Column A. And the number of columns in your worksheet will remain the same, regardless of how many columns you delete, add, or move around. Think of columns as location information that is actually separate from the data in the worksheet.

Rows

Rows run down the side of each worksheet and are numbered starting at 1 and up to a very high number. Row numbers are also locational information. The first row will always be numbered 1, the second row will always be numbered 2, and so on and so forth. There will also always be a fixed number of rows in each worksheet regardless of how many rows of data you delete, add, or move around.

Cells

Cells are where the row and column data comes together. Cells are identified using the letter for the column and the number for the row that intersect to form that cell. For example, Cell A1 is the cell that is in the first column and first row of the worksheet.

Click

If I tell you to click on something, that means to use your mouse (or trackpad) to move the cursor on the screen over to a specific location and left-click or right-click on the option. If you left-click, this selects the item. If you right-click, this generally displays a dropdown list of options to choose from. If I don't tell you which to do, left- or right-click, then left-click.

Left-click/Right-click

If you look at your mouse you generally have two flat buttons to press. One is on the left side, one is on the right. If I say left-click that means to press down on the button on the left. If I say right-click that means press down on the button on the right.

Select

If I tell you to "select" cells, that means to highlight them. You can either left-click and drag to select a range of cells or hold down the Ctrl key as you click on individual cells. To select an entire column, click on the letter for the column. To select an entire row, click on the number for the row.

Data

Data is the information you enter into your worksheet.

Data Table

I may also sometimes refer to a data table or table of data. This is just a combination of cells that contain data in them.

Arrow

If I tell you to arrow to somewhere or to arrow right, left, up, or down, this just means use the arrow keys to navigate to a new cell.

Cursor Functions

The cursor is what moves around when you move your mouse or use the trackpad. In Excel the cursor changes its appearance depending on what functions you can perform.

Tab

I am going to talk a lot about Tabs, which are the options you have to choose from at the top of the workspace. The default tab names are File, Home, Insert, Page Layout, Formulas, Data, Review, View, and Help. But there are certain times when additional tabs will appear, for example, when you create a pivot table or a chart.

(This should not be confused with the Tab key which can be used to move across cells.)

Dropdown Menus

A dropdown menu is a listing of available choices that you can see when you right-click in certain places such as the main workspace or on a worksheet name. You will also see them when you click on an arrow next to or below an option in the top menu.

Dialogue Boxes

Dialogue boxes are pop-up boxes that contain additional choices.

Scroll Bars

When you have more information than will show in a screen, dialogue box, or dropdown menu, you will see scroll bars on the right side or bottom that allow you to navigate to see the rest of the information.

Formula Bar

The formula bar is the long white bar at the top of the main workspace directly below the top menu options that lets you see the actual contents of a cell, not just the displayed value.

Cell Notation

Cells are referred to by their column and row position. So Cell A1 is the cell that's the intersection of the first column and first row in the worksheet.

When written in Excel you just use A1, you do not need to include the word cell. A colon (:) can be used to reference a range of cells. A comma (,) can be used to separate cell references.

When in doubt about how to define a cell range, click into a cell, type =, and then go and select the cells you want to reference. Excel will describe your selection in the formula bar using cell notation.

Paste Special Values

Paste Special Values is a way of pasting copied values that keeps the calculation results or the cell values but removes any formulas or formatting.

Task Pane

On occasion Excel will open a task pane, which is different from a dialogue box because it is part of the workspace. These will normally appear on the right-hand side in Excel for tasks such as working with pivot tables or charts or using the built-in Help function. (They often appear on the left-hand side in Word.)

They can be closed by clicking on the X in the top right corner.

About the Author

M.L. Humphrey is a former stockbroker with a degree in Economics from Stanford and an MBA from Wharton who has spent close to twenty years as a regulator and consultant in the financial services industry.

You can reach M.L. at mlhumphreywriter@gmail.com or at mlhumphrey.com.

* * *

If you want to learn more about Microsoft Excel, check out *Excel Tips and Tricks* or one of the main Excel 365 Essentials titles, *Excel 365 for Beginners, Intermediate Excel 365*, or *102 Useful Excel 365 Functions*.